Tin Cat Alley…and other poems

Mark A. Murphy

ISBN: 1-7349469-5-6
ISBN-13:978-1-7349469-5-6

Ever tried. Ever failed. No matter. Try Again. Fail again. Fail better. –
Samuel Beckett

CONTENTS

Table of Contents

Foreword

Back in 1996 when *Tin Cat Alley* was first published by Spout (a small, independent English publisher) one reviewer wrote that 'it would be a shame if Murphy was overlooked by the big publishers.' Quarter of a century later, he is still looking to branch out and find a wider audience for his work.

Nonetheless, the themes, preoccupations, and questions proffered in *Tin Cat Alley* are still relevant to today's readers. By releasing Murphy's first chapbook along with *Other Poems: Not to be Reproduced,* we hope we can reignite the early confidence in this poet's work, and broaden his appeal to new generations of poetry lovers.

In addition to the original thirty-seven poems, this new collection offers another sixty-nine previously uncollected pieces.

Tin Cat Alley

25th Anniversary Edition

Tin Cat Alley…and other poems

to

Helen Bullas, whose exuberant confidence in Tin Cat Alley
is my only claim to the epithet, poet.

My sincere thanks…

The Lead Cat

I am the quintessence of the age.
I am the lead cat. I am not afraid to speak my mind.

Stand up, I say. Stand up for what you believe in,
if you believe in anything at all.

No matter it's no longer fashionable .
No matter if it offends certain sensibilities.

Ladies and gentlemen, hold on to your carats.
No matter if talk of goodies and baddies is purely subjective

or if what's said is not even listened to.
And no matter, especially so, if what's said
is not even considered poetry.

A record run at the iceberg has dealt us a cruel blow,
the cruellest blow of all. Here are your greedy ship owners

making a last mad grab at immortality.
Here is John Jacob Astor, buying up stock and real estate

waxing his stiff upper lip. Thinking
the unthinkable.

No matter, even now, if what's what, isn't necessarily
what it seems. As the ship goes down,

and the final eulogies are spoken, each must face
the inevitable gurgling alone.

Weighing on the mind like lead, an inquest
or two million knock-off rivets.

Din. Din. Din. Din. Din.
What a ridiculous notion: A titan made of tin.

Mark A. Murphy

for Bruno S.

…so, your car's kaput, and your girlfriend is gone,
and thine house they have sold…

It is important for poets to talk about loss
in their poetry
whether it be lost love, the loss of reason, or the
loss of hair.
We might observe, then, that losing, by whatever
margin,
is fundamental, not just for poets, but for all of
us.
By the same token, without loss, nothing can be
gained.
A penny that is never lost can never be found.
A man who has never lost at poker will only know
what it is like to win. In virtue of this, he has
lost out

on what it is to lose.

Alas, the balding man pipes up, anxious to be heard,
posing his question, before any eventuality of him
losing
his thread: But does all loss have equal weight?
And we must do him the decency of addressing
his enquiry. After all, to the balding man, hair loss
might signify the loss of youth, virility, or even
his position
in the world. For him, the experience of balding
might well be commensurate with our horror
at the fat woman on the cliff face, an inexperienced
climber,
who, by some misfortune has lost her footing
and now dangles by her own unfortunate shoelaces.
Even as I relate her story, the audience voices
their dissent: Dolt! Dullard! Dunderhead!
Has she completely lost her marbles?

As for the man who has never lost out
in love,
we might well conjecture that he too is lost.

The Untrodden Snow

A girl in the pub thinks I'm a poet.
She asks me what I do.

I tell her I notice things,
like her mouth, its thick lips.

She says it isn't good enough.
She wants to know what poets do (she has her own ideas).

Mainly they live in lofts,
eat baked beans straight from the tin, drink a lot

and can be seen, more often than not,
walking in town parks.

She says it's all part of their job.
Last night, I was drunk, walked home through the park,

didn't see her there, didn't see anybody,
just some snow drifting this way and that

and a dog barking at a tree.
When I got home, the whole street was in darkness.

The snow was all mine.
It felt good thinking about the girl in the pub.

How open she was. How her whole body smiled.
How her teeth betray beauty

as the whole pub lit up. Her laugh when she said:
I think poets are supposed to write poetry.

Manageable Space

Anyone acquainted with the ideas of Herr Freud
will be glad to learn as I did,
that we are not alone in our anxieties.
Even the good professor suffered
bouts of agoraphobia
which is no laughing matter,
since the response is one of terror.
Asked what it was that caused the fear,
he might have said it was his childhood,
an early memory of steam trains,
the action of the pistons,
or that the rattling of the carriage mimicked death.

Imagine then, a lake or reservoir -
nothing too disturbing.
You are standing at the water's edge.
You see yourself from a great distance.
What do you see but a human dot?
You need to get away from the water, the expanse
is too much, too blue.
You need to get back to the world of enclosure,
the world of manageable space.

Now imagine Sigmund's train.
On such journeys the mind is lost.
The reasonable world is lost to the opening out
of an unfamiliar landscape -
hills and mountains, estuaries and flood plains
where the desire to get free
is contradicted by the desire to hide.
At last, you can put yourself in the shoes
of the good professor.

Mousetrap

She doesn't look very happy standing there in the
rain.
I feel uncomfortable, watching her through the
blinds.

I've got things to do, besides she doesn't need my
sympathy.
Maybe I should call to her, lend her an umbrella.

You'd think she'd have one, dressed like that in the
rain.
Then again, it wouldn't do. I mean, who'd be
interested

in a girl trying to keep dry, when it's raining cats
and dogs?

Fragile Spring

for Katrina

The Chinese flower seller is selling spring,
in pubs and clubs, at all-night parties.

To couples in stifled rooms, who are hoping,
the boys to give, the girls to receive -

a bit of spring. She tells them
words are not enough, flowers are needed.

Yes, it is spring she is selling, on city streets,
in urban gardens, emptied of feeling.

And the lovers who are falling,
they are not alone - grasping at fragile spring.

"Crocuses! Daffodils! Tulips!"

Notes from Prison

for Osip Mandelstam

I read your poetry at night. I am a big fan
but what of the Opposition
at Vorkuta. Who will sing for us?

You're insistent,
St Petersburg is a grave for the intelligentsia,
but the whole of Russia is a grave.

A knocking-shop of death. Who will join
the choir of frost for the faithless
applause? Who'll kneel for us as the squinting Sun
pleads

with the sky. I speak to you after years of silence -
there is no River Camp mine.
No speechless spring,

No re-education. Only the heavy crunch
of departing feet in the snow - forced marches
into the tundra, and the criminal 'goodbye.'

We've gone beyond the pall
of prison gates. Prison poplars, and writing in
holes.
Yesterday never existed. There's no red court.

No red Czar. No bending of art.
No clean bread. No final words for fools.
Only wind in the red banners, enemies of the people,

and the noise of time. Osip Emilievich,
I know your darkness.
I've lived it in my own little way.

Night Bird

From this room, there's no telling
what you can see, the dereliction of mills,
is only part of it, too familiar
to be considered important by passing
buses or cars. Go tell it to Oscar
or Nancy, or a hundred moons taking refuge
in the rafters, where air vents are secretive
like hooded monks, mumbling prayers.
You've lived in many rooms,
but none like this, none as revealing as this.
A thousand dreams made of tears
in the morning light
as you wonder how much of this is true?
Do you see the red sky at night
with the eye of an artist, tracing the dark of the sun?
Have you forgotten the river's tears
when you look us in the eye
and the new moon punts on the Thames.

Do you still dream of playing the Moonlight
fantasia, outside the Bodeleian
for Miss Lonely Hearts before morning lectures,
or do the dreaming spires
dream you back to your lonely room
in Old Headington?
When we begin again,
remember how we forgive and blame.
How the shadowplay of voices,
rids the room of curtains that only keep us
in the dark.

Fly Story

The fly in the fly bottle won't play today.
Perhaps it's too hot. Everybody knows
it's not good to be cooped up in such heat.

Even the boy crawls under the iron bedstead
to where it's cool. From there he can hear
his parents shouting, but doesn't listen.

He's proud of his captive, but can't help
wishing it was a butterfly, better still,
a caterpillar. If only he catch another
to keep it company, to keep it from dying.

He hits the glass bottle with a rusty nail,
bangs it against the wooden skirting.
It's not fair having to be in for nine years old.

His mother shouts for him to get to bed.
School in the morning, and something about
a bloody-good-hiding. He stops.

What if the bottle breaks?
The fly doesn't move. He taps the bottle
and waits. The weather's hot.
The night undisturbed. Not even a breeze.

Years later, he recounts the story drunk
to the woman he's living with. She's upset
by his lateness. He crawls into bed.
She can't go on like this. He doesn't move.

Mark A. Murphy

Notes from the Apparatchiks Desk

The new regime has ordered the removal
of Vladimir Ilyich, from all public places.
He is no longer regarded as a friend.
From now on, we shall refer to him as Lenin -
less than human. A monster like Stalin.

Remaining portraits are to be stripped
from all government buildings and incinerated.
Portraits of President Yeltsin
will replace them. Statues will be
dismantled, by brute force if necessary.

Certain books will have to be burnt.
No point arguing. Certain books
will always have to be burnt.
It's a busy time for the new bureaucracy,
the renaming of parts is not for mugs.

A spade is no longer a spade.
It is a shovel. Government directive No. 53.
Laugh at us and you'll be disqualified
from entering the state lottery.
Laugh with us and fortune will surely be yours.

In our efforts to rediscover the past,
the Lenin Brain Institute
will have to close. You will remember -
we do all this, not out of love
but in the name of progress.

The new authorities have revealed
that Lenin's brain - was only marginally
bigger than average - a matter of ounces.
Hardly surprising, then, that
70 years of research have been in vain.

The Tobogganist

I'm finished

with God. I never wanted to be
favoured anyway. It's not a question
of faith, being abandoned or even fallenness
from being. Dasein is only another way
out, an abstract prop, improvisation
for the stage. Let me tell you,

being encased in ice isn't much fun.
Too much time to think.
Obsession with death is nothing
new, only gets you down. It's remembering
always remembering. The mountain
doesn't concern itself with the weight

of the avalanche. Don't get me wrong -
I embrace the physicality of the world.
And though it's dark down here
I dream a lot. Sometimes I dream of monks
in monasteries where the air is thin.
I have questions of uncertainty for them.

Being well versed in the doctrine
of eventualities only hampers the process.
Nevertheless, I dream of girls
and lots of them too, but the best times
come in quieter moments,
when I think I can see the winter sun climbing

among peaks and glaciers.

September in Paris

Il n'est pas certain que tout soit incertain. - Blaise Pascal

September rain fingering the cobbles
outside Café de Flore.

Night air suffused with tomorrow's bread.
Saint Germain full of couples being couples.

Already, I'm lying but the lie pleases
because the lie is all that is left.

I can't help myself. Call it human failing.
My particular failing. The need

to know, thirsts for answers. The night-
no longer than it ever was.

Just less involved. All the same, the sky
tonight is heavy with clouds.
And my reaction is agoraphobic.

But this isn't your problem. For you,
the problem is 'indifference.'
You, the perfect Stoic,
with your arguments against laughter.

How could I forget the woman
on the fire-escape, rubbing sun lotion
into her thighs.

I need to know the lives she's involved in,
the rooms she might live in.

Yet I pretend I'm only interested
in the distance from A to Z.

Look for the common denominators.
Be confident. No matter that your teachers
thought you innumerate. Two and two
never equalled four. O we know it's useless.

All that's certain is our manipulation

of these distances. Our exile self-imposed.

September in Lyon's Tea Shop.
The sky over Huddersfield in ruins.

On the Nature of Discourse

Polemics in Marxism are common-place,
the discord only natural.
So, it's adequate to note
that Professor Burnham opposes

Marx's dialectic on the grounds
of crude determinism. And with it
the historical necessity
of anything, especially socialism.

When asked by Professor Novak:
Don't you think you will die someday
and isn't it absolutely necessary
or do you think you might be immortal?

Professor Burnham replied
with logical consistency:
My death is not absolutely necessary
and certain, it is only extremely probable.

Poem Towards the Acquisition of Patronage

Queen Elizabeth, it's the same old story,
my mistress has left her husband and taken off
with another woman. The age of chastity
has surely passed and the waiting millions
are still not happy. Queen Elizabeth,
old certainties have given way to rumours
of scullery maids who call you Brenda.
Won't you dish the dirt on austerity
by throwing more Maundy money at the poor.
Queen Elizabeth, I'm not that well up
on court etiquette, but your Anus Horribilis
is cropping up on everyone's tongues. It's time
to celebrate the great unwashed,
who only live to see the erotica
in your private collection. Queen Elizabeth,
here it comes again, like an intruder
in a royal bedroom or cousins who marry
in the national interests…

I'm just an old-fashioned boy
who can't say no-
my heart's in a terrible spin.

Footnote

Always, and in all ways, we are by ourselves.
Yakov Sverdlov

In modern Russia, there is talk of restoring a Tsar.
The surviving Romanov's wait
with bated breath, mesmerised by their sense
of fate. Throughout Europe duty calls.
All the old houses are waiting.
The little boy, Grand Duke Giorgi, is no exception.

What must he make of it all. His ancestors shot
by the Bolsheviks. The seventy years
of communism. And now this, his grand tour
of Ekaterinburg. What must he make
of the commotion in the square.
The brutal words of his Cossack defenders.

'Sverdlov shot the Tsar! Pull him down! Kill him!'
Once again, the sky is darkening
over Ekaterinburg. The Eastern Orthodoxy scatter
holy water and incense before the guns
of the riot-police. The would-be Tsar,
little Giorgi, can only look on, bewildered by it all

like an orphaned princess praying for the divine.
Yakov Sverdlov, looks on unmoved by dynast, duchy
and Divine Liturgy.

Moveable Feast

In St Peter's Gardens, the youngsters sunbathe
on the well-kept lawns. Office girls hitch their skirts up,
rub protective lotion into their thighs. Passers-by pretend
not to notice, but the workmen in their plastic hats
on the church scaffold, whistle and grunt between bites.

Round the edges, the paths are paved with gravestones.
Some of the names are indecipherable. I wonder if, anyone
else has noticed, how soft the ground is?

Notes from the Art Underground

It's said, that Van Gogh's ear could distinguish the sound
of sunflowers rustling from the sound of irises -
even at twenty paces. It's said, that the chattering
of irises, is something to write home about.
If you sit quietly enough, you can hear them growing.
It's said, that the ear still mourns for Gauguin
and Gabrielle Berlatier. That loneliness
is all in the mind. That Van Gogh's mind was unstable.
And the ear although elusive in later work, found
its way into the post, time and again.
Ladies and germs of the jury, the ear was famed
for its lonely disposition, yellow skies and blue fields.
But when you turn the lights out, colour dissipates,
like the handsome cousin that you would kiss,
or the farmer's daughter, who takes her secrets to the grave.

All the same, sitting in the dark can be just as revealing.
It's well known, some of us prefer it that way.
This at least is certain, it is easy to feel your way
round a piece of sculpture. Who hasn't had their paws
on the arse or tits of a bit of marble or bronze.
It's well documented in the history of sexual fetishism.
Inanimate objects are known to induce orgasm.

What's less easy to accept, is moles listening to paintings.

The Grinder *after the painting by Diego Rivera*

for Keith

Grind. Grind. Grind. Always grinding.
Love, don't you see how thick my arms have become?
I have worn the stone to a gentle curve
with my thick arms. A stranger
in my own back yard. Always kneading,
never needy, while you court the rebel youth
with tacos and tequila
on the front porch, talking with your comrades
and poets (a revisionist bunch,
the lot of them) about your revolution.
Emiliano, don't you see how rough my hands
have become, and me the eldest daughter
of one of the finest families
in Guadalajara?

My dress, the only dress I own
is in tatters, so much so, that I'm afraid to show my face
at market. Every day I straddle the worn stone,
my arse in the air to the prevailing winds,
and all I hear is your talk of the people.
What is to be done and why. Who the friends
of the people are, and infantile disorders!
How you belong to the people,
how your people will provide bread for the people
(with their hands out) until I'm at a loss
for what to think.

Grind. Grind. Grind. Always grinding. My love,
I grind for you and the revolution.
He who has the youth
has the future, but these tropic nights
when I lie awake,
exhausted by the day's debates,
I can't help but wonder, who really has the future?

Woman in the Green Jacket

after the painting by August Macke

Our lovely Edwardian virgin certainly looks striking
in green. However, one needn't be dismayed
or feel irreverent that our virgin still dreams
of being taken in the silence of the rhododendrons.
And who could blame her? After all, the question
lingers on all our lips like the effulgent gossip
of washer-women at the mangle, the necessary ontology,
and figuring of grief - will the tinker ever return
as promised on that fateful day by the lake,
when he pushed his luck under the picnic blanket.

Not to mention his hand, beyond the call of duty,
and the deliberations of petticoat-love. Over and under
into the green yonder of folds, of that magnificently
buttoned green jacket?

La Belle Romaine

after the painting by Amedeo Modigliani

I can't listen a moment longer to your theories about adultery,
your ramblings about love. The world of intrigue no longer exists
for me. I won't get on all fours, not even for you, Modigliani,
not even for the sake of art.
Every day we perform these rituals, the same childish games
but today is different. Today I come to the studio a stranger,
a refugee in my sandalled feet, bleeding little puddles which drain
through the floorboards.
Poor Modi! The pretence is finally over! Picasso has left me
for a girl called Jeanne and all I can do is run. I'm running away
from this city of artists and lumpens, where schoolgirls, are all too
easily fondled into bed.
I used to love Paris in the Autumn, but now the rain has lost
its charm. No amount of rain can assuage the city's bored tears
or the mess I now find myself in. The rain is lost on both of us
and we're both lost in the rain.

At night, I dream of the river gurgling through the
city.
I see it from the studio window washing through the
streets
of Montmartre. I'm alone in bed and the Seine
    is collecting debris for the sea.
When I wake up, the sheets are soaking. Some nights I
feel
as though I'm drowning. Such is the nature of
departures!
Such is the nature of love! Old love departs for new,
    new love for old, or no love at all.
Sometimes it just departs. Unsure of everything, like
the concierge
in her high chair on the floor below, watching the
water drip
from the ceiling, seep through the cracks in the
wall,
collect in puddles at her feet.

The Gypsy Lovers

after the painting by Otto Muller

Love's young dream courts perfection by the lake.
Understanding little or nothing
of transience, they embrace and kiss
playful as children under the linden trees
on the edge of the forest.

Though there are no row boats on the surface
or for that matter, any discernible water
in the painting - it all exists
like amaranth or instances of joy -
without refrain or the need for qualification.

They would not have it any other way.
He gives her the stars, she gives him her thighs.
We cry in our various renascences:

'Love is not love unless it hurts!'

Woman in a Fish Hat

after the painting by Pablo Picasso

We're well acquainted with your public life,
inside us all the terror is waiting.

The private tragedy we do not talk about.
People and places we cannot share.

You're right, scars never mend. They grow
less visible. Seem less real. Days run

into one another
like paint. Grey into black

but we remain inquisitive. We want
to know more. We want details.

You say it's not possible. It cannot be said.
And we're sad because you've fallen

silent. Your hands knotted
as if in pain. Your breasts struggling

under canvass. Under the weight of that fish hat.

Tixall Road

This is my present to you. A painting
of a man and woman, in a rented bathroom.
The man is shaving.
The woman washing her hair.

Each day the past month, I've lugged
the image of it from pub to pub
in my drunkenness. Talking all the while
to strangers about oil paint
and poetry. I say to them, imagine
yourself there in the painting,
among the whitewashed walls and pumice.
There where the breeze cools
the water's skin, hardens breasts
and nipples. If only you could see it now,
the goosebumps and the sun
pouring all day.

If only it wasn't wrapped up like this,
awaiting the final touches.
You'd see how peaceful the scene is,
how simple.

How unlike worry.

A Bigger Splash

after the painting by David Hockney

Nothing moves in the eleven o'clock sun, not even the
splash.
It is July and the deckchair casts the self-same
shadow
it has always cast. Beyond the east-facing windows,
everything
is certain. The palm trees out back do not anticipate
wind.
The grass stationed against the east wall of the
apartment
does not expect rain, nor do the windows ever expect
to be opened.

In the blue geometry of water and sky, the matrix of
flatness
and suspension denies feeling. There is no
impropriety,
no leaves in the pool, nothing doing except for the
splash,
meticulously detailed. And so, it is, only the splash
with its eternal whooshing that makes the implausible
possible.

End of History

The party leadership extol the virtues of the west.
They appeal to the people, arms outstretched,
their hands held as if in prayer:

To get rich is glorious!
We must learn to swim in the ocean
of the commodity market!

In the distance, tanks move over the cobbles
like cattle.

Chips with Bits

Caught between the tired looks
of a woman too busy
to smile, and the queue:
longer than usual for this time
in the evening. A boy
of twelve, choking on the smell
of beef fat. Sickened
by a poverty, he thinks unique-
mocked and bullied
by children, telling him it is.
Seeks his reflection
in the polished steel of the counter,

and hates.

Diogenes Searches for Foundation

for David Morley

Sceptics say the window is intangible.
I don't doubt it. Modern alchemy (science
if you like) is the stuff of fairy tales.
However, I'm blameless. I never pretended
any progress towards truth, the window
is only a nightmare for the sleepless,
dependent on, yet independent of the subject.

Forget history. The invisibility of the atom
is at stake. I only excavate the past
to rid myself of worthless artefacts.
To prove my point, I've given up the barrel
for a room of glass, not nearly as comfortable.
I can't deny the difficulties involved,
the nights of research leave me glassy-eyed.

And though my dreams have become disturbed
since I took to dreaming syllogisms,
the results are quite satisfying. Up to press,
I've found there are three types of people
in the world - those who throw stones
at lab windows, those who don't
And those who're permanently skating on glass.

Of course, there are set-backs, the unconscious
mind is reluctant to allow for valid logical form.
Last night, I stumbled on a world without sand,
a world without windows, wild flowers, grains
of any description. Then the dream shrank
from me, and I woke in a glass room, no bigger
than a demijohn, no more significant.

Mark A. Murphy

I could go on for an age like this, except
the critics are crowing about testability.
I must get back to my step ladders, chamois cloths
and random variables. I can’t keep away
from the window with its lack of certainty.
How, if shattered, it might resemble the universe -
broken glass, spiralling down in infinite regress.

Prometheus Depressed

Okay, I'm downright morbid at times,
especially just before breakfast
but what do you expect,
with that damned bird preying on me
all the time. And the sea,
the damned Aegean, forever spraying salt
into my wounds.

(His mania rings out over the cliffs).

I'm sick to death of this bum deal.
Sick to my stomach of waking
every morning with the vulture at my liver -
it's knackered anyway.
O' Fortuna! Empress of the world!
Who really cares
about the suffering of others. The gods.
Don't kid yourself.

My one regret: I only wanted to be normal.

Uncle H

It is quite possible then, that uncle Hector, deceives himself
with visions of love (trinkets, amulets, photographs - all junk)

all of it carried from pillar to post - the assemblage of a secular life.
When what he really sees, is the fallen ankle of obsession,

bleeding in its sandalled glory, bloated on the field of regret.
Lying, lying, lying like weathered bone, anaemic

against the whitening sky. That's uncle Hector alright. Always one
for the grand negative. Poor Uncle H, busy creating his own

disturbance, stares at his shield. Abandoned in the sedge.

Threnody

Despite Ariadne's protestations
on Hector's behalf, vis a vis the Minotaur's
habitual hunger - good words are hard
to come by- and Hector knows this
primarily, because the heart
of the Minotaur (whose business really
is eating princesses) isn't easy to come by.

Despite all the known facts about what is
reasonable, it's reasonable to believe
that one will NOT be gobbled up for breakfast -
by a beast half-man, half-bull - the Minotaur
(the bastard) simply can't find it within
himself to be reasonable.

Minotaur Fabula

i

The Minotaur isn't all monster
but a poet at best.
An hunger artist, at worst.
At odds with an uncaring world,
and cruelty for cruelty's sake.

Remember to take him at his word,
for a creature of habit
is only good
as his word allows.
Remember, for every doubting Thomas -
a philosopher gets a hard on.

ii

The Minotaur isn't all piss and vinegar.
The Minotaur is a creature of conscience.
The Minotaur isn't all sucker for love.
The Minotaur is a glutton for punishment.

The Minotaur is, after all, half-human.

Uncle Hat Knossos

I have dreamt all the best poems, never written
them down, except the odd line scrawled
on the walls of the labyrinth.
Never the chance, met most days by the sound
of builders and labourers busying
themselves with bricks and mortar, as the wall
is raised ever higher, until thoughts
of escape, return once again to thoughts
of enclosure. This is my world
of sensory deprivation. Walls and parapets.
Parapets and walls. Where touching hurts.
Touch is alien. Yet it is touch alone that counts.
And the poem written is like Daedalus
regretting the decision to fly.

Orpheus in Love

i

Caught once again calling her name.
Caught once again with his pants round his ankles.
Caught once again wishing for her return.
Caught once again asking the obvious.
Caught once again berating the cruel fates.
Caught once again unable to sleep.
Caught once again lamenting the fact.
Caught once again tossing salt over his shoulder.
Caught once again with his head in the jar.

ii

Poor Orpheus! Pilloried by his contemporaries,
who, in the main, remain sober… (staring
into the abyss). Stop crying over unfair reality! It exists
the way it exists! And you'd do well to bloody well
accept it! But our hero (pitiful in his loss)
being rather sceptical at times, asserts that reality
no more exists, than the fears of what we cannot know
or the drinks for which we cannot pay
and simply won't rest until Eurydice is restored.

Goddess! Nymph! Girl of nineteen years!
What man wouldn't feel it in his bones - love repeating
itself in a photograph of time, first as tragedy,
second as farce.

iii

Alas, poor Orpheus (punch drunk as a paradox)
loves what he cannot love, lives
for what he cannot live, and will no longer sing,
since all his singing is given to doubt,
drinks himself stupid at every turn like a man caught
once again in an antonym of boozy devotion
and treachery, self-sacrifice, and self-immolation,
heartbreak and overindulgence.

Kojack Eulogy

This is not Kojack.
This is New York without any hope
    of resurrection.

This is a poem then, without lollipop love.
This is New York breaking away,
floating away into the Atlantic towards Europe.

This is the new world meeting the old.
This is New York without any sense of solidarity.
    Who loves you now, baby?

This is New York meaner and tougher than ever.
This is New York bleeding to death.
No one can sleep easy in their beds.

This is a poem for Kojack. A lament for Jacques Derida.
This is the trash can of history accepting
the impossibility of meaning.

    This is New York.
    She is dressed in black.

    Kojack is dead.
    She is inconsolable.

Funeral Party

When the hours of morning stop and death forces its hand,
the dead will come to your bedside as strangers.
Carrying their mirrors like lanterns. They'll gate-crash
the skulls of the heaviest sleepers. Leave them
with nothing. Want nothing. Not even regret. Hear this.
I'm the last guest to leave. The last chief of the gooney birds.

Mindful of my responsibilities. Mind full
of excuses. Listen to the sea for no other reason than it's there.
Listen so long as listening matters. I have strayed
a thousand miles off course. Left my nesting grounds
to the stone men. And come among you to let you share
my sense of loss. Hooray for the excesses of the ego.

I want my fifteen minutes of fame. My prints on the side walks
of Hollywood. Cut me and I bleed. Peck at me
with your beaks. Peck at these eyes until they're blind
as the sun. The problem remains. Half-four.
The sun at its brightest lights the room, demands meaning.

Ceremony

Walking the hours into morning
hoping that rain could displace regret,
the further I walk the more obvious
it becomes, if there is a constant
it's the knowledge that you're not
coming back. I'm like the man
on the road-gang waiting for the rain to clear,
the man on the platform wanting
to jump, arriving early, hoping
the train will be late.
I rush into a phone box with no one to call
and nothing in mind except relief
from the rain, only to find
the air rotten. I could argue
the phone was an enemy
to communication. But it doesn't matter.
Tonight, I can't deal with ghost
conversation. I've finished
with self-justification and the dividing
of blame. It could've worked
and then it couldn't. One last poem,
that's all I wanted to give you,
one last poem with regrets too numerous
to mention.

The Tin Cat

We are at war, me and the cat with the kids next door.
If you hadn't already noticed, I'll spell it out.
My cat is made of tin. It has red fur and black eyes

and not the other way round. It lunges at passers-by
and nosey parkers. And isn't in the least bit superstitious.
The neighbours think there's something strange

about a kid with a lump of tin but the joke's on them.
We don't care what they think. All morning we've been diving
through their privet hedge for fun, making holes

while they're out at work. Our philosophy is simple.
They've had it coming for ages. Like I said, tin cats are the best.
They don't like nosey parkers because nosey parkers

are like mice. And they don't like other cats,
especially cats in poems. This is Tin Cat Alley. Keep out,
if you know what's good for you.

Other Poems: Not to be Reproduced

Tin Cat Alley…and other poems

"Everything we see hides another thing; we always want to see what is hidden by what we see."

Rene Magritte

Acknowledgements

Agony Opera - An Old Hut on Baildon Moor, Between The Wars, Beyond the Beyond
Arcs Prose Poetry - Larks Ascending Haibun, Sunday Haibun
The Bookends Review - At the Crossroads
The Bosphorus Review of Books - Moonlight Sonata
The Dawntreader - Port Enyon, Reprise
GloMag - Helen I - Helen IV
Gone Lawn - Phantasmagoria Haibun
Guinevere Review - Catastrophism
Grand Little Things - Bardsey and Beyond
Ink, Sweat and Tears - Old Haunts
KNOT - Innocent Blood
The Literary Yard - Critique of Critical Criticism, Rhetoric and Prosody
Muse Pie Press - Leveller, Walking Out, Walking In/Between the Wars
The Paddock Review - Lethal Loneliness
Peculiars Magazine - Magical Thinking
Plum Tree Tavern - Eater Walk
Poetry Pacific - Snow Dream
Poetry Repairs - Snow Dream
Runcible Spoon - Beach Shadows, Dilletante
Scarlet Leaf Review - Meaningless Haibun, No One Gets Out of Here Alive
Shot Glass Journal - Leveller, Helen V, Glasshouse
Sonic Boom Journal - Obsessive Ruminations
Synchronised Chaos - Magical Thinking
Tuck Magazine - Gentrification, Clayton Fields, Condolences Haibun
Truth Serum Press - Walking Out, Walking In

In lieu of a Preface…

Other Poems: Not to be Reproduced

Most of the poems in 'Other Poems: Not to be Reproduced' chart my relationship and preoccupation with my friend (now my oldest surviving friend) proof-reader, editor, critic and 'one time' lover, Ms. Helen Bullas.

Helen became the dominant muse in my work between 2013 and 2019. Without her support and encouragement, I don't think I would be writing this preface today, publishing this, or any other book.

All souls love, hurt, feel lonely and weep. All souls embody the infinite. And so it is, we reach out to connect and reconnect, not only to one soul but a billion souls at once.

It is my enduring hope that any would-be reader might find the time to join us on this happy/sad journey into the interior.

Ancient History

If you were a forest,
I would be shafts of moonlight falling
upon you like a secret

If you were a mountain,
I would be the dawn monsoon falling
    upon you like a kiss

Between the Wars

I cannot be
all things
to all people

any more than the moon can illuminate
the paths between us, or the heron
be magnanimous to the carp.

Before long the cracks begin to show,
the house falls in to ruin,
the old dog cannot scratch its tail.

Now I must betray my love,
which ultimately involves lying to you
in that Bombay garden, we only dare dream of.

Walking Out, Walking In

Not just one footpath, but many paths
as we pass white flowering blackthorn

shouldering holly, hawthorn and elder.
Past the age-old dance of wild borage

and blue and white honesty propagating
along the roadside. Through field and stile

into cerulean woodland beyond design.
Far beyond the serpent's head of beech

and broken backs of last year's bracken.
Where the ballet of this year's bluebells

plays itself out under a canopy of oak,
birch, and the enchantment of bird song.

Moonlight Sonata (1st Movement)

There is a moon, that rests in the quiet corners
of a lover's lips. -
Sanober Khan

What matters most to lovers is silence,
the hungry space between
the 'little deaths,' which last an eternity -

the place where we find the fragments
we piece together
as if to restore time, the infinite

balance between birth, living/dying
and being reborn in the stars.
Only moonlight knows the hesitation

between loving and longing,
grief and our inability to give ourselves
without recourse to doubt.

But moonlight on the waves moves us
like the motion of tides
rising and falling within the heart

as we indulge our fancies -
the act of love echoed in the adagio sostenuto,
the interval between kisses

delicately strung, silently
unfolding - night flowers softly embracing
(forever) between two chasms.

Pluviophile

It's raining in the almost forgotten doomsday village,
beating down on St Mary's tower,
filling the guttering which overflow with joy
whilst a local man tears open his shirt

and dances on the dry earth, soon to be quenched
by the summer storm. He remembers
stories of old monsoons and imagines living
in a rain forest where he might hide

from his peers and swim in blackwater rivers
where the daily downpours would renew
and awaken in him a lost innocence,
that he might smell the ground and trees once more

and cry out to the gods: *this is the day I've dreamed*
all my life, this be the day it rained forever

Bugle Call

Strange how the world appears
so ordinary,
except for your inability
to swallow - every breath arrested

as the Sour Apple melts
on the tongue,
leaving what remains of crushed ice
to filter down the windpipe

which is closing, rapidly now
as you make your way
to the infirmary
to see the consultant orthodontist.

*

His only injunction, upon finding
the open abscesses -
an ambulance to theatre
where a specialist will perform

a 'Life-saving' extirpation,
before inducing
a coma, enabling him
to place you on a ventilator in the ICU.

*

Now, you will dream for a week
of Bubble-gum Slush.
Unaware
of the collective will,
after the towering inferno
tears at the very fabric of the vertical village,

consuming doors, walls, cladding,
and people,
as cell phones transcribe
confessions, pleas,
messages of love, and last uneasy breaths.

Critique of Critical Criticism

for Martyn C.

Anyone au fait with the ideas of Professor Bloom
will find nothing fortuitous in their return
from the dead, disagreeable
though they may be, as a dose of the pox.
Who really listens to the discourse of canon makers,
sanguine, as they are, those champions
of the literary big talk -
denying access, once again, to the plebeian poets,
who lack 'cohesion' in the parlance of love
(archaic and moribund, boorish and confessional)
voicing their dissent
at the city limits, outside the seats of learning?

Should we turn a blind eye
to those acolytes of critical criticism, or note
with all due attention, the 'inability to resolve the tension
between the lyrical and erotic'
in a given piece of work? We ruffians, all,
might well declare such solipsist observations
as phoney, thinking as we do
that the learned man is out to double-cross or bamboozle.
For us, neophyte poets, laymen and women
of the thronging masses,
the moon might yet bring woman to man,
despite the 'reservations' of the academic heavyweight.

Would the Sterling Professor, the son of a garment worker
in the Yiddish speaking Bronx
and Orthodox Jew, care to tell us why
the poor infant in the Favela (in all likelihood)
won't grow up
to be a canonical poet?
All influences aside, no one knows, categorically,
why we write, or what is ultimately meant
by taking one symbol over another,

only that those pale Nordic tits might well bring comfort
to the (in)famous and the damned,
though the egoist (Harry Bloom) clearly will not die -
but remains unflappable in his patrician conceit.

O'Connell Street Bridge

We know that frown, we own it
having lived it for years
too numerous on the clock. Father

and son, strolling along
O'Connell Street, on pilgrimage
home to Kerry. We wonder

what their conversation
might've been, knowing little
or nothing of that time,

only that father didn't favour
his tie, and Grandfather
gave a shilling to one barefooted

beggar boy at the ferry port
for hauling their luggage
across the city. Our Grandfather

looks soberly into the distance,
Cornelius junior squints
quizzically into the Dublin sun.

The scene is set for historian
and poet to reconcile past
and present with the ghosts

of O'Connell Street - benign
and innocent. Our father,
all of seven years in age,

and his father, lost in thought,
photographed strolling across
the bridge in their Sunday best.

Pale Blue Eyes

After dinner, we talk of the old days, times
when we were free, when we were lovers.
Did it occur to us then, there would be a time
when one might fall again for the other?

I may as well tell you, as I make my way
to the confessional, I have begun to fall for you
in ways I thought were no longer possible.

But you will not be won by me or any other man
as we discuss the shifting sands of our lives,
both agreeing that my advances should stop.

Perhaps our longings are best expressed in song,
but it hardly matters during times of defeat
when the heart is full of longing, except to say,
'linger on your pale blue eyes...'

The Persistence of Adrenalin

for Oli

We look out of death’s window
both picturing our own ends
out on the road below.

Today the vituperative adder will eat the blue jay’s
eggs
without any thought for tomorrow. Disquieted by the
strange
unreality of falling, we each in turn panic at the
thought of it.
Then the news you've dreaded all week - cancer has
finally taken your aunt. What can I tell you, my
friend, except,
cry your heart out whilst you can? Tonight, death’s
window
will call to us again, beckoning like a beacon of
heaven. And
we will resist temptation, slowly but surely,
learning more
each day how to avoid senseless pain.

Today the black bear will not save the raven from a
watery grave.

A Moonlit Lane with two lovers by a gate

If you don't control your own life, somebody else will. -
John Atkinson Grimshaw

Imperceptible. Almost entirely consumed
in shadow - two inscrutable lovers
declare their undying love

in the late autumn moonlight
on a lonely wooded lane. The only sign
of any other life at all are the deep impresses

left in the road by horse and cab ferrying
the nocturnal lovers from city
to suburb in the small hours

before dawn. Nothing quite so quixotic then
as that first kiss on a moonlit night
evoking care beyond telling

where the old gate, and silent leafless trees
act witness.

Not to be Reproduced

Life obliges me to do something, so I paint. - René Magritte

Poet. I have seldom read you, but I have seen
something of the infinite abyss in you.
Strange, how I talk to you now, as if in limbo,
studying the silence that envelops you.

One can't help but wonder what's going on
in that beleaguered, surrealist head of yours,
two years ahead of the war, three years ahead
of Trotsky's assassination in Coyoacan.

I'm not certain if what I see is a portrait
of a poet, or the mind of a genius.
When I look at the back of your head
in the mirror, I struggle with writer's block

to say anything more meaningful than:
Ceci n'est pas une pipe, which really translates
as: 'This is not a portrait, but a lesson
in portraiture, as much as it is a lesson in life.'

I wonder if you agree with your painter friend
that art is equal to the mysteries of life?
Like René, I conceal nothing. My only hope
is to look the abyss in the face without prejudice.

Fledglings Behind an Iron Gate

Have you seen them, the two tiny fledglings, trapped
and chirping behind the wrought iron gate?
I walked past them only this morning, thinking
of their doom, though the diminutive mama bird
would beat off all comers in any eventuality of an
attack.

I wonder if there's anything I can do to help,
but nothing seems possible. Here we have two
flightless
birds, fallen from the eaves, grounded, unaware
of imminent danger, though they call and call
to their mama for the sustenance only she can give.

Too bad these creatures have fallen to their ruin,
no one can tuck them back into their nest.
So, our lives unfold, hardly moving at times,
only we flew the nest decades ago, despite
our misgivings, and any inability to cope alone.

Now the neighbourhood bullies will have their say
and our fledglings will undoubtedly perish.
Much like you and I, they can't live by love alone,
and though we would welcome them into our house -
death must have its fancy throughout the godless day.

Yin Yang on Baildon Moor

We spy the winter sky
through gaps in the shrunken boards
as we rouse from our dreams.

The embers in the cast iron stove
still smoke and moan
in the languid morning air

as we stir and waken in the cold.
Soon it's time to heat the kettle
and toast hot-cross buns

for breakfast before riddling cinders
and ash to enliven the fire.
Strange how we find our selves

in the middle of the moor, miles
from the nearest conurbation
or bus route, enamoured

by the simplicity of Ling, Bell
and Cross-leaved heather, disarmed
by Kestrels hovering on the wind

not nearly found in town or city.
So, we drink our fill of Jasmine tea
out on the veranda, watching

Red Grouse run wild among the sheep.

Aladdin Stone

You give me an Atlantic beach pebble.
Smooth as your skin.

Decorated with red love hearts.
Paisley and human eyes.

When I touch the stone under my pillow -
it might as well be your breasts.

I touch the Jasper now to conjure you.
Your net of light.

No One Gets Out of Here Alive

One day you find yourself alone in A & E. Your throat so constricted
that you can't swallow, or breathe to save your life. At this most
unpropitious of times, you make your request to the operating surgeon.
In the event of my passing: Do Not Resuscitate.

There's no self-pity in this resolution. Only a sense that you don't want
any more pain. You wish, in some way, to control your own demise.
You have no choice about being born, but no one has the right to inform you
of when it's your time to go.

When you're dead, you're very, very dead.

Before and After

A perfect rain falls,
washing away our mistakes,

past loves, defeats,
decades of hurt.

So, love grants another
reprieve and we steer clear

of the abyss in favour
of shorelines and mountains.

This is how it is with us
as we take to the sea

remembering to forget
memories of pointless death.

Phantasmagoria

Curlews call out across the evening sky.
The team in the ICU are talking about death.
Certainly, this is no place to expire.

The beds perform a death rotation,
as we each move further down the queue,
nearer the death lane, the last leg of the journey.

We can't say it's all been bad, wasted passion.
We're all in the death queue, though not all
are in the ICU. Most pass peacefully.

But not us. We're caught in this death rotation
and we're dropping like flies. Now the nurses
are talking about who will be next.

Outside, the curlews won't budge an inch.
We're waiting for the death rotation in the ICU
and the curlews are singing their little hearts out.

Phantasmagoria Haibun

It is entirely possible that the Brahmin doctor in the ICU (having lost her patient) is out to kill you, take your life for his. The heady mix of final chemicals flooding the brain is enough to render you delusional. You are unable to rationalise your exit. The nurses are discussing your options. Now the ward team are voting on life or death.

You figure at least three of these bastards want you dead. You hear them conspiring in the ward. You are too weak to move. One nurse pleads on your behalf. This man is too young to die. He is from a poor family. His parents can't afford to bury him.

The Brahmin doctor is preparing to administer a lethal injection to stop the heart. Now there is nothing left but to force the brain to stay awake until morning, watch the vultures close up, as if in a dream.

The pewits are in full voice outside the ICU. Calling on you to leave.

Beyond the Beyond

We have already passed, 'I dare you.'
You are both dared and daring.

I wonder if you think me strange
as I think you strange.

We rearrange ourselves, as we walk.
You ask me if I love you?

We embrace in the rain. Holding
on to each other for dear life.

As if will alone could determine it.

Codex

Beneath my hands, your breasts
harbour the lost coda

of dreams, where secrets
and orphans wander

along the shorelines of desire.
Wherever you move,

I hear the sound of the sea,
and I'm spellbound,

because we're together
and all your flesh is kissing

my flesh as the dawn pulls
all our hopes in concert.

So, wave falls upon sand
and the mist falls away

in the sun, shifting all reasons
for loving off-kilter.

Only, we're dreaming again,
and kissing inures us against failure.

Helen I

When you look into my eyes,
you see how beautiful you are.

Helen II

When I look into your eyes,
I see how beautiful I might be.

Helen III

A yellow wag-tail skims the surface
of the old mill pond, searching for insects.

For two whole days, we've been rapt
in each other's company, weighing the odds.

This necessary event draws us up short
as we remember Hodgkin's paintings

with all their necessary urgency of colour.
So, you hold me within your light,

casting your net out wide, as if to keep me
from falling, head first into darkness again.

Helen IV

We love in the shrive light
as if we'd been given a last chance.

Going On

Imagine Time as a symptom of being in love.
You choose how fast or slow you move.
You cling to the things I've written,
moving you off your centre, dislocating you.

I tell you, it's only temporary, come back home
and you well up with tears, but don't cry.
Now is the time to build new bridges,
release the balloons in a daring act of celebration.

The old anecdotes paint an unbalanced past,
my past without you and I feel ashamed.
Soon enough, we will challenge our
notions of Time Lost as a symptom of Being.

Soon enough, we will find ourselves in that
other Eden where we'll pick our fill
of apples and berries, remembering then
to kiss as though kissing were to be outlawed.

Wanderers

You possess me as I possess you
as the Seven Sisters wander
in the night sky waiting for our

next encounter, our unspoken
lovemaking. Momentary distance
aside, we wander together

in our dreams, as if we could never
part. You follow me to a clearing
in a wood and we kiss as if kissing

was our natural state. We feel
the pulse of the river in our blood
chasing shadows, as we trace

each other's bodies with our mouths.
Soon we will take flight with
the rising sun hoping for renewal

before wandering into the sea.
Now we hear the voice of the moon,
a prayer in passing pulling us back

to ourselves, our ancient love.

Simnel Intimacy

Beyond father and son, beyond
faith, and the taste of almonds
dipped in tea, we pass over

the pack-horse bridge at Eastergate,
where sudden waterfalls flood
across the moor. So, we draw closer

in wind and sun, past the iron
gated goddess, and moss-covered oak
as if to reinvent the wheel of fate.

Now our earlier reticence
gives way to a new sense of union,
as the trunks of willow divide

and proliferate along the bottom
of the dyke, where we navigate
clumps of bramble, aspen and ivy,

through the last of the Easter rain.

The Lovers II

No ordinary lovers. No ordinary kiss.
Though our faces are hidden from view
we coalesce more each day,
dreading the moment of our unveiling.

Not that we have anything to hide,
the artist had us pose this way -
everything you see hides the infinite.
Our love is invisible, but ever-present,
the alternative to this is not loving,
which is no alternative at all.

What can we show you with a kiss?
The eye hardly remembers,
only the heart holds the memory of it.
The rest is dreamscape and mystery.

An Old Hut on Baildon Moor

It's raining hard on Baildon Moor. We came here
today to make soup and watch the butterflies
dance in the rain. Like us, they wish
for shelter. Like us, they're alive to the possibilities
of the flesh, wild and somewhat slightly dazed.

We kiss through the afternoon and our kissing
robs us of our defences as we stumble and swoon
across the creaking boards to the bed.
Now the light filters in through gaps in the walls
and we capture our fleeting recollections

of the Bandstand that brought us to this place
where long ago we danced and dreamt
as children of our future lives. We never guessed
then we'd end up here, counter-balancing
our two realities between the pots and pans

and stove where we would prepare dinner.
So, the divinities of place seeps into our bones
as we're mesmerised by the sound of rain on wood,
and the laughter of the brook as it challenges
Swallowtails, Red Admirals, and Purple Emperors.

Leveller

Turn the timepiece on its head. Watch
time, the great enabler,
allowing the harvest of innocence.
A timely kiss. A timely prayer.
Offering a way in. Demanding a way out
of one romantic time-line
(many lifetimes ago)
in favour of an older, timeless romance.

Turn the hourglass on its head. Watch
the woman and the girl
you fell in love with running home late.
And not out of time.
For future time is what she dreams.
Time-wise, but not time weary.
Synchronising the local time on her wrist
with the Greenwich Mean Time on her phone.

kingbird

(for M.W, P.R & G.H)

it was in another century, we asked
too much of you,
we asked for the moon, the meaning of the stars,
but you were hardly treading water yourself

you said the human creature was the highest
expression of matter on earth,
you were wise beyond your years, except with women,
but we were never sure

you said I was the 'soul of chivalry' - we
have not forgotten,
one score and ten years of exile are enough for any
man

let's welcome you back now, old friend, unsadden the
heart,
we shall sit on that fraternal veranda together
and watch the mourning sky

Going Home

If I could kiss away all your pain, I would -
because being with you
is the nearest thing to being home.

Now I am too sad for words.

Word Painting

A poem is not clay, it does not appear out of the ground,
any more than you or I
appear out of the ether. We craft our hearts out of lino,
knowing that love does not need to be written, crafted,
or otherwise talked out, because love like innocence, calls
our names out loud, in the fleeting air.

Helen V

A yellow wagtail declares its presence
in the stream, hopping from stone to stone

with a whistle and a song as if to grab
our attention. We wonder what locale

it is from? Could it be the same bird
from an earlier poem, searching us out?

Certainly, things have changed, our bird
isn't searching for insects this time

and we're not searching for love
because it already resides in the sound

of the stream rushing over the rocks
and the sound of the breeze returning

in the highest branches of the tall trees.
We sit on the veranda surveying the scene,

writing, communicating our ideas, while
the bird preens itself in the morning sun.

Gift

Two weeks to your birthday.
The cold in the flat entices me to write

as if the act of writing
might chase out the winter chill.

When I think of you naked in bed
losing all sense of propriety,
it's a wonder I'm not gone mad.

Each time you turn, I follow you
as you follow me, and we see

the world beckon in its entirety,
and for the first time, I'm not afraid.

Morning near the End of August

(i.m. Glenda C. for Trevor, Pat, et alia)

When I think of you, only laughter
comes to mind, as I recall the many times
(over half a lifetime ago) we shared

a Black Velvet or Diamond White
in the student refectory before
and after class. We must've thought

then we were quite invincible, and certainly
more street, or savvy than our fellows.
Now we can only dream you back

but our memories are young as ever,
young as you always appeared
with your energy and aquamarine eyes.

Old as we are, wise words are nothing
but bits of dust, debris of spider's webs,
the dust of life, and we professors

of arachnids come here now to dig
the living earth, and anoint you before
your next journey to the stars.

Our words are used for so many things
but now we must use them to say
'farewell.' Your shadow passes across

the window and we're grieving,
but there are so many words for grief.
Grief belongs to each one of us alone,

each one reaching out beyond our limits
waiting for the leaves to turn, stirring
silent as moths in the night air –

nothing solid as we thought it might be.

Mutability

What is she doing out here in the suburbs, so far
from her woodland home, surveying the yard next door?
Perhaps she hungers for worldly things,
human yards paved with gold?

Oh, we know, she is no magpie, and still
the nude silver-birch loves her kind
as we love them both in their kindnesses.
Our tree a constant friend through seasons thick and
thin.

The wood pigeon, a one-time visitor to these parts,
where man covets man
in the long struggle of the flesh,
for goods and power over his neighbour.

What shall we call her this early morning, perched,
as she is, in our favourite silver birch,
quite remarkable in her winter finery, feathers
plumed
against the cold?

Some names are forgotten in time, some deeds good and
bad
pass us by, but the simple act of a bird feeding
in our favourite tree as she passes by
is just enough to make the morning worthwhile.

Reading Eliot for Agnes

Helen has been reading
'Prufrock' all week, and we feel
obliged to mention it here,

though no one really cares
beyond Helen
and her Quaker friend, Agnes.

*

When the landlady calls, 'Time,'
as she must, we must
all consider Time

before the next round of forgetting.
Dead hands. Dead losses.
And dead ends.

*

Nonagenarian, Agnes, knows
this only too well,
but still favours the payback

of silent reflection
to Prufrock's tortured confession.
And, or, the society
of the dead.

Prayer to the Immortal Wind*

I see a darkness…
like a second death coming… Gone…
like the red-backed shrike
  from the Brekland fens,
gone as well, the Corn Crake with its song
from the grasslands and hayfields of England.

Gone the Kentish Plover from sandy coasts
and brackish inland lakes - where our loved ones
play in the sun - innocent as daylight.

Gone too, the Great yellow bumblebee
like the Large copper butterfly before it.
Gone the long-familiar way of the brown bear,

grey wolf and wild boar, beaver and lynx,
wildcat and Great Auk. All extant.
All departed from Blake's green, idyllic land.

*

O immortal wind!
Hear the mournful verse
of bird, bee, and beast!

Restore all of Nature
before man's destruction
of the living Earth…

that we might fly, swim and rove again
in summer sun and winter rain,
on foot and wing, without disdain.

---

* England's animals and plants have been going extinct at a rate of more than two species per year for the past two centuries.

Towards Understanding

Father is drunk once more, singing
in the garden, gazing up
at heaven,
the starry constellations
as if looking for answers in a god

he doubts exists. A child watches
in an upstairs window
taking care
not to be seen.
What must he make of his father

singing songs and reciting poetry?
Only the echo and abyss
of self - an explosion
in the four-chambered heart.
Now a grown man, it seems the past

has not entirely passed us by.
Just when was the hourglass broken?
The enchanter
is drunk in the garden.
The son could not hold his eye

even if he wanted to. The past beckons
like a journey into the interior -
where life and death
vie for ascendancy, in a life-time
of quarrelling, poised between truth
and illusion.

Meaning(less) Haibun

What we are running from, or to, is hard to say,
but we're all, more or less, running
in the same direction. Certainly, we humans
are adept at running away -

down the street,

up the stairs, to the end of the road, towards devilry
and damnation, since beatification is not an option
for the many. So, we move through the fair
with an air of desperation. Only, the garish lights,
speeding carriages and smell of fast food
is all too much to take, so we begin to run again
headlong into the next debacle.

Sometimes faith abandons us, and we are like children
again, searching for meaning, except we find we are
meaning less each day, and wholly meaningless at the end
of days, given the scope of our local universe
and Godless abandonment.

Meaninglessness is both
blessing and curse
when living a deadly lie.

Robin's Regret

Now it's high time to let go
    of the past,
and not before time, since time is running out,

challenging any impulse to remain, overwhelming
our obsessive in a deadly game
of take and taking, where the blue robin's eggs

are stolen from the nest with no thought
of tomorrow's fledglings.
So, we build our dizzying walls, only to watch

the great edifice toppling to the ground
every night in our dreams
where we walk on rivers of ice,

perched regrettably between the living
and dead, offering nothing
but long-ago memories, as if memory could save us

from bottle and pill, the daily dalliance and gamble
with death, eating at heart and mind
in a last-ditch attempt to rob any and all humanity.

Unbearable Lightness

Not really surfing, more like standing still
in the sea
until the surf challenges
your ability to stand steadfast, or maintain
your balance

in the face of the dynamic swirling undertow,
which energizes
both mind and body
in ways, you hardly remember, like loving
out of season,

or returning to a much-loved book
in which heroine
and hero find amity,
before writerly high-jinx or wisdom,
finishes them off

in an unexpected crash whilst driving home,
emboldening
you to stride out
into the open expanse of water and wave,
as if hoping

against hope, you might yet start over.

Beach Shadows

Footprints and shadows. All we know
or dream is here. The assemblage
of secular life writ large upon the beach.

Defining and redefining past and present.
No windows to the soul. Nothing to see
or guide the eye, beyond two silhouettes.

Watching the waves, advance and retreat.
Hands reaching, across time and sand.

Glimpses of the Godhead

At first glance, we appear as survivors
of yet another schism, storm, or cuckoo's conspiracy
-
flailing wildly in the rabid air
in an age of public outrage and doubt. Pilgrims
searching for tomorrow's gods, beyond
the bolted door, and deadly tides weaving
catastrophe.

In one instance, we're friends, and the next, half-
blinded,
unable to feed, throw the dice, or mend the fence.
Slaves to our compulsions, unable to see
sun or cloud, load the brush,
settle accounts, or stroll leisurely homewards
in hope and favour of some Sunday afternoon sobriety.

So, we collapse time, stay in bed, throw away the key
to the shackles. Only, we're self-aware,
wearing our chains lightly enough
to fool the godhead into believing
we're free. When, in fact, the moon conspires and
nails us
to our own commonplace crosses.

Now we live out these numberless days, seeking
assurance from the wind. Borne
on white wings, high
above moor and meadow. Renouncing sorrow.
Enduring in craggy folds. Embracing the root and
branch
of love. Resolute in our affinities.

Amsterdam

Cities always have that effect, dividing
the young from the old.
So much for the old man in black
out to peddle some verse.

No mind to the endless girls thumbing
their knickers down,
or the Baristas slumming it
in yet another break from reality.

Here's where it hurts you the most,
amid the tram stops and bicycle lanes
where the fashionable ladies
pedal to yet another deadening score.

The Return and Retreat

I've just been organising the last five years of
poems
that I wrote for you. I didn't expect that I loved
you
as much as the poems called out, yet I remembered
your shadow on the beach at Aberdaron, where you
met your match in the Atlantic water, wave jumping,
relishing your time in the surf, like a cat dreaming
up
mischief, snatching worried fledglings from the nest.

Now the waves shroud you in a rainbow of seawater
as if to welcome you back home, and your laughter
can be heard back on the beach, purifying the sea
breeze, ringing in the warm air like the church bell
at Thomas' last ministry, where nearly thirty years
of love's disrepair, are effaced within the concord
of silence, drawing us closer within the worn-out
walls.

Why I Write

To shew the fly the way out of the fly bottle
because we all have to be flies at one time or
another

To bring you place names like Port Enyon
and Aberdaron
because you bring me apricots in the morning

To leave you with the names of stars like Vega, Rigel
and Alpha Centauri
because you never leave me hanging in the cold

To find meaning beyond God and the vastness of space
because we're all small beside the large oak

To let you know we could drink Summer wine together
    one day
because we do not carry drunkenness in our hearts

To share certain words like certain moods
because you deserve only care

To greet you with poems when you wake in a morning
because your acts of love leave me speechless

Devil's Rock

Evening in Spring Wood
Silver birch, cool to the touch
Spring water trickling
through rock as we wander
Every door opening
between wood and river

Owls swooping in the rain
spitting in the dusk
putting paid to the devil
We step closer for a kiss
on the granite bluff
Under a blaze of stars
Trembling before we depart

The Revelation of Opposites

I feel the weight of you as you sit balancing
on my knees in front of the computer
playing songs by gay Paris' Little Sparrow.

Your body lithe and almost weightless
like a small boy, but for the weight of emotion
emanating from your voice as you sing along,

translating the words as you go: *Toi...* You...
Toujours toi... Always you... *Rien que toi...*
Nothing but you... *Partout toi...* Everywhere you...

*Toi... toi... toi... Toi...*You... you... you... You...
Now I'm convinced. As far beyond doubt
as the moon, which radiates its light

into every corner of our evening, igniting in me
the paradise of femininity, the realisation that
your love for me is as obstinate as mine is for you.

Je t'aime... I love you... *je t'aime à en crever...*
I love you to death... Irreducible. Harmonic.
The artfulness of the absolute. Heavy as time.

Dilettante

No easy passage. The earth hard and frozen.
What do we do when we're not making supper?
Our lives are so very different.

You are moral, perhaps the most moral being
I know. I have made nothing
possible, only a life of alcohol and longing,

ways to hide when the frost starts to sing.
I have ignored all the calls to prayer,
my only communion, that with my comrades --

a lifetime ago. Between dilettantism, misadventure
and trips to the pub, I have spent my waking
hours brooding over one luckless woman

after another, until confining my search to you.
Now our differences are posed, poised,
predetermined to rent us apart.

What do we do, Helen when we do not do?

At the Crossroads

In search of light and love and lost time,
the months are flying by
faster than either of us imagined.

Loneliness speeds us to the grave
more surely than disease,
yet we remain impotent in the face of it.

Try as we might to cling to the past
and each other, the present
has a proclivity for mass murder.

Wind swept and shell-shocked, we stand
on different shore lines,
ineluctably alone, defying the odds.

Our fates inextricably bound, written
by fear and solitude,
unerringly devoted, waiting around to die.

Subverting Emptiness

An early morning owl shrieks
in the low branches
of a monkey puzzle tree - its calling

wholly insistent
for the time of day, and me being
rather superstitious

sought the noisy creature out
as if my life depended
upon it.

Age-Old anxiety really, this calling
of birds
piercing the dawn,

my suspicions,
my suppositions,
my doubt.

Arrogant to think this fellow
had anything left to say
to me, but I listened intently,

all the same, heading towards
my first half-century, as if
to heed an ancient admonition:

get out whilst the going is good, and don't look back.

All Maps Welcome

Just when you thought it was safe to come back
in from the cold, retrieve the milk
from the doorstep,
open the mail amassing behind the door -

you wake up, as if from a dream
where worry meets you at all points of the compass.
Just when you thought you knew
the way home in the dark, the reasons for betrayal,

and who your real friends were - you fall
into the thorny hedge
and must crawl the next twenty yards to freedom
through a thicket of twisted twigs and bramble.

Just when you thought it was safe to go back
in the water, tide and current advance
in a marriage of fear
and longing insisting upon another drowning.

Just when you thought you'd hit rock bottom,
you find yourself alone (the last man alive) grieving
on the lower ground in the Chapel
of Rest, one floor above the hospital mortuary.

Just when you thought her memory could sustain you
and love would never end -
the night gives way to the dawn chorus
with all its chattering, guilt, and dead ends.

Woundology

Sometimes the wound is so deeply etched, wrought
upon our bodies so profoundly
like poison ivy cutting in, garrotting the tall elm
that we hardly dare move
from the dining table, for fear of further reprisals
in the unguarded moments
between showing and telling, where a mind can be
forgiven, for reliving a past trauma,
or asking forgiveness, long after forgiving ceases
to matter for the wounded child.

So, the rabbit in the headlights freezes on the
frozen moor,
where we ourselves have trod -
before being crushed in some bloody oblivion.
And the wounds we live with, and by God
hide, from our families
and loved ones, have a way of growing ever more
luminous with every passing day -
press-ganging us into the confessional,
in the hope of forgetting the wreckage that lies
at the nexus of every human soul.

Murphy's Razor

Blood stains the page.
Commas cry ideological tears.
Cuts bleed into you.

Where will it end?
We are not entirely sure.
Only this is clear.

For now, we are apart.
When the end comes, bloodlessly
or otherwise,
I want you beside me.

And into eternity we will fly.

Ashkenazy plays Chopin Nocturne in C sharp Minor (No.20)

I have enough burned-out stars tonight
to fill my suitcase and depart
from your house into the heart of the city.

Every key struck rends the cheeks with tears.
An implacable sadness overwhelms
my rented rooms; the dream

of our younger selves is nearing an end
neither of us conceived, the blood
moon rides high in the January night

and we are each alone in our different ways.
Pity goes the way of stardust, as we listen,
impatient now, for a last reprieve from the piano.

Small Dragon

There's a pain in our hearts
keen as fire and steel.

Centuries old, waking alone
in darkness.

Worrying over the lost
decades, snapshots of children.

Now, we think of love
like a resolution

to soldier on, without a home.

*

No use to sit and meditate
in silence, deny

or avoid the dragon's claw
or burning breath.

There's a pain in our hearts
we can never escape.

Autumn Equinox

The moon lives in the lining of your skin. -
Pablo Neruda

No time to lament
autumn's retreat.

No room large enough to hold
all our kisses. What we might do
but for the pitfalls of a life lived

without caution. So, we steer
away from the past, as if time past
might still hold some peculiar fancy.

Now the moon plays match-maker
again. Coaxing us to re-set the clocks.
Draw up balance sheets. Re-draw

the map of the heart. Leaving us
to pine. Watching moon shadows
dance in the abandoned bandstand.

Yellow Moon

You come as its coming dark
Hair newly coiffured

A parcel of grapes, and Earl Grey

We stand two metres apart
Passing time
You running late for dinner

Both running out of seconds

So soon time's up
All that's left a last embrace

In less than a minute
we'll be strangers

No time to catch a breath
The words on the tip of the tongue
Helen
Do not go
Do not go this time

Sky glowing yellow with grief

Drawing the Curtains

No iron-curtain, separating nations -

but curtains of heavy calico
cleaving inner and outer worlds,
creating the dichotomy
between plain talk and tall story,
trust and disbelief.

Where one account ends, the other
is just being born, dividing us
further - as if you might even favour
your concealment -
from where you look out

to see if the darkness still consumes
everything in sight.
Like discord between east
and west - the heavy oak pole
through which the eyelets are threaded -

hangs regrettably from its thread (jutting out)
from above the window
as if it could fall
at any moment - abrogating any notion
of loving (for loves sake).

No iron-curtain, just converse beings
attracting and detracting.

Missing Persons

Bring me the drowned leaves
from the beck,
that we might transplant them

to where my heart should be
in this ritual losing

where you walk
with your son and friends,

defining yourself in the clear
Grasmere water
thinking of our summer trysts.

*

In some other world
far from well-worn paths
'a mother of three'

is found naked
hanging
from the low branch of a tree.

*

Listening to the night wind
in the high sycamores,
it is you alone -

you alone
I spy
on the open fells.

Bardsey and Beyond

I am alone on the surface of a turning planet. -
R.S Thomas

When sun and moon align, and the spring tides peak.
You might recall our walk along the cliff tops,

and the reassurances you gave against falling
as you cast your net of light, over both land and
sea.

Sorry to think how the tide has turned on sentiment.
Strange how refuge turns so suddenly into chaos.

No boat to ferry us to the island of saints and
pilgrims.
No last crusade to cement the bonds between us.

High time to say goodbye to the bogus world of
bodies.
Nothing left of kindness, beyond the heart's stubborn
failure.

Afterthought

Larks Ascending Haibun

Outside history. Outside the clouds lowering upon this ward.
What do we have here, but INNOCENCE and DEATH? Try as we might,
to react to every lark, every breeze makes us lighter. For we are each,
and all, valuable to the next, as we are to each other.

The birds in the trees have no knowledge of Doctor P. Yet he has
saved so many lives. And we must pay tribute to a man, so selfless in his
devotion.

Lights. Lights in the night. Riders and rovers. Voices. Voices
in the night. Sirens and setbacks. This is our maddening destiny.

Remember the names of those who care. Jasmine. Lisa. Max.
Raj. Ben and Paul. Those brave men and women.

Helen, we say unto you…

THANK YOU
for
edifying INNOCENCE
eluding DEATH.

www.ingramcontent.com/pod-product-compliance
Lightning Source LLC
Chambersburg PA
CBHW030414310726
48979CB00002B/412

* 9 7 8 1 7 3 4 9 4 6 9 5 6 *